We Work! Animals with Jobs

Seeing-Eye Dogs

by Jenny Fretland VanVoorst

Consultant:
Bonnie V. Beaver
College of Veterinary Medicine
Texas A&M University

BEARPORT
PUBLISHING

New York, New York

Credits

Cover and Title Page, © Boris Djuranovic/iStockphoto; 4–5, © The Sun, Benjamin Hager/
AP Images; 6–7, © Lars Christensen/Shutterstock; 8–9, © Don Farrall/Photodisc/Getty
Images; 10–11, © Richard B. Levine/Newscom; 12–13, © Juniors/SuperStock; 13, © Casey
Christie/ZUMAPRESS/Newscom; 14–15, © RiverNorthPhotography/iStockphoto; 16–17,
© Ragnar Th. Sigurdsson/age fotostock/SuperStock; 18–19, © William Mullins/Alamy;
20–21, © Boris Djuranovic/Shutterstock; 22T, © RiverNorthPhotography/iStockphoto; 22B,
© The Sun, Benjamin Hager/AP Images; 23T, © Lars Christensen/Shutterstock; 23B, ©
Prentice Danner/iStockphoto.

Publisher: Kenn Goin
Creative Director: Spencer Brinker
Design: Craig Hinton
Photo Researcher: Arnold Ringstad

Library of Congress Cataloging-in-Publication Data

Fretland VanVoorst, Jenny, 1972–
  Seeing-eye dogs / by Jenny Fretland VanVoorst.
      pages cm. — (We work!: Animals with jobs)
  Includes bibliographical references and index.
  ISBN 978-1-61772-894-5 (library binding) — ISBN 1-61772-894-2 (library binding)
  1. Guide dogs. I. Title.
  HV1780.F74 2014
  362.4'183—dc23

2013008477

For more information, write to Bearport Publishing Company, Inc., 45 West 21st Street,
Suite 3B, New York, New York 10010. Printed in the United States of America.

10 9 8 7 6 5 4 3 2 1

Contents

Meet a Seeing-Eye Dog

Meet Max.

He is a **seeing-eye dog** that helps Ann, his owner, stay safe.

Why does Ann need Max's help?

Ann is **blind**.

She depends on Max to help her get around without getting hurt.

A Great Team

A seeing-eye dog and its owner, called a **handler**, work as a team.

The handler, who is blind, cannot see things in his or her way.

The dog, however, can show its handler where to go.

To do this, a seeing-eye dog wears a special **harness**.

By holding on to the harness, the handler can safely follow the dog.

6

harness

Helping on Stairs

Seeing-eye dogs lead handlers around so that they do not fall or trip.

For example, the dogs are trained to stop at staircases.

By stopping, the dog is telling the handler to be careful.

The handler then knows to use extra care when taking the next step.

9

Crossing a Road

How do handlers cross busy streets without getting hit by cars?

Their seeing-eye dogs help them out.

The dogs stop at street corners so that handlers can listen for traffic.

When the sounds of cars stop, handlers know it is safe to cross.

The dogs then lead the handlers in a straight line across the road.

Taking a Bus Ride

A seeing-eye dog can also help its handler ride a bus.

a seeing-eye dog at a bus stop

At a bus stop, the dog waits with its handler.

When a bus arrives, the dog walks up to the door and stops.

Then the handler knows to be careful as he or she climbs on board the bus.

Going Places

A seeing-eye dog learns how to guide its handler to nearby places.

For example, they may go to the library several times together.

This helps the dog remember how to get there.

The handler also teaches the word *library* to the dog.

Then the handler can say, "Take me to the library."

The dog will safely lead its handler there.

a seeing-eye dog leading its handler across town

What Makes a Good Seeing-Eye Dog?

Most seeing-eye dogs are retrievers or German shepherds.

These dogs are smart and friendly.

It is also easy to train them to avoid danger.

For example, the dogs quickly learn when it is not safe to cross a road.

The dogs refuse to move so that the handlers know to wait.

Training a Seeing-Eye Dog

At special schools, dogs are taught how to work with handlers.

As part of their training, the dogs are brought to noisy or crowded places.

After a while, the dogs learn to be relaxed and calm there.

Now they can pay close attention to their handlers.

trainer

Always on the Job

A seeing-eye dog needs to pay attention to its work.

It wears a vest that lets people know that it is working.

Do not pet a working dog unless its handler says you can.

After all, a seeing-eye dog has an important job to do!

20

Glossary

blind (BLINDE)
unable to see

handler
(HAND-lur)
a person led by a
seeing-eye dog

22

harness (HAR-niss) a handle that a seeing-eye dog wears so that its handler can hold on to it as he or she is safely led around

seeing-eye dog (SEE-ing-EYE DAWG) a dog that is trained to lead people who are blind from place to place

Index

Read More

Bozzo, Linda. *Service Dog Heroes (Amazing Working Dogs).* Berkeley Heights, NJ: Bailey Books (2011).

Hoffman, Mary Ann. *Helping Dogs (Working Dogs).* New York: Gareth Stevens (2011).

McDaniel, Melissa. *Guide Dogs (Dog Heroes).* New York: Bearport (2005).

Learn More Online

To learn more about seeing-eye dogs, visit
www.bearportpublishing.com/WeWork

About the Author

Jenny Fretland VanVoorst is a writer and editor of books for young people. She enjoys learning about all kinds of topics. When she is not reading and writing, Jenny enjoys kayaking, playing the piano, and watching wildlife. She lives in Minneapolis, Minnesota, with her husband, Brian, and their two pets.